Art Safari

To Parents and Teachers:

Welcome to The Museum of Modern Art. This guide is an invitation for you and your children to explore the collection of painting and sculpture together and make your own discoveries. Rather than providing information about art, this book encourages you to learn about artworks by looking and talking about what you see. The questions proposed in this guide draw upon children's natural curiosity and eagerness to share their ideas. Some of the questions help children to describe what they see. The questions at the end of each sequence encourage children to think about the artists' intentions. The at-home art projects help children make connections between what they see in the Museum and their own lives.

This guide can be used to explore art with children in the Museum, at home, or in the classroom. Orient your children to the *Art Safari* theme by reading the introduction. When visiting the Museum, explain to your children that it is important not to touch the art or the walls. Then discuss the eight works of art featured in this guide. The location of the works in the galleries changes from time to time; ask staff at the Lobby Information Desk or a security guard for assistance in locating the artworks. Explore at your own pace, discussing the artworks that sustain your children's attention and enthusiasm.

Some information about the artists is given in the At-Home Activity boxes. If you would like further information about the Museum's collection, listen to the audio guides, visit the Edward John Noble Education Center on the main floor of the Museum, or consult the Painting and Sculpture Collection Pages at www.moma.org/collection/paintsculpt. Keep in mind that children often have more fun and learn more by talking about what they see rather than by being provided with historical facts, names, and dates. Think of *Art Safari* as an adventure in looking and a time for listening to each other, and enjoy.

Children and adults are also invited to write stories about animals in art and create fantastic creatures at *Art Safari* online at www.moma.org/artsafari.

Joyce Raimondo
Department of Education
The Museum of Modern Art

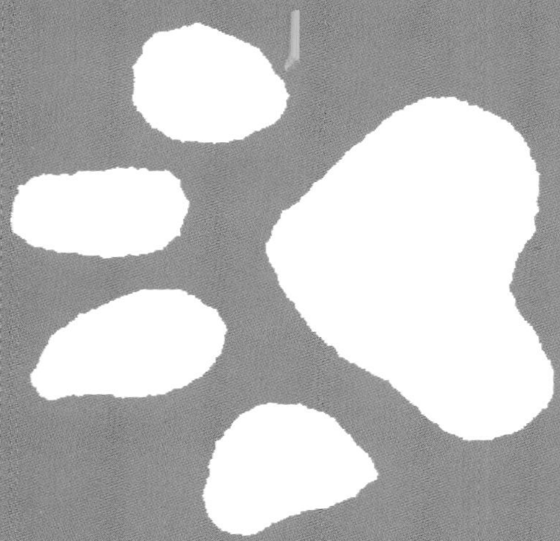

Art Safari

An Adventure in Looking
For Children and Parents at The Museum of Modern Art

By Joyce Raimondo

The Museum of Modern Art, New York

This publication is made possible by grants from Agnes Gund and Christina R. Davis.

Produced by the Department of Publications
The Museum of Modern Art, New York
Edited by Rachel Posner
Designed by Arpie Gennetian Najarian
Production by Amanda W. Freymann
Printed and bound by Tien Wah Press, Singapore

Library of Congress Catalogue Card Number: 97-70263

Third printing, 1999

ISBN 0-87070-059-6

Published by The Museum of Modern Art
11 West 53 Street, New York, New York 10019

Printed in Singapore

Cover: *The Sleeping Gypsy* (detail). 1887. Oil on canvas, 51″ x 6′7″ (129.5 x 200.7 cm).
The Museum of Modern Art, New York. Gift of Mrs. Simon Guggenheim

All artworks illustrated are in the collection of The Museum of Modern Art, New York.

Introduction

Today you are going on an Art Safari. A safari is a journey—an adventure in looking. During today's safari, you will search for art and look for animals in paintings and sculptures. Once you find the work of art, look at it and talk about what you see. Look for clues that help you figure out the stories in the artworks. Who are these animals? What are they doing? Where do you think they are? Why do you suppose the artist made an artwork like this? Remember, there are no right or wrong answers to the questions in this book. Learn by looking and listening to each other, and have fun!

What's going on in this picture?

What do you think the lion is doing there?
What kind of personality does the lion have?

What can you tell about the woman lying next to the lion? Who might she be? What do you think she is doing?

Where do you think the woman and the lion are? Explain.

What time of day or night do you think it is?

Look closely. There are no footprints. Can you explain this mystery? How do you suppose the woman got there? And the lion?

Do you suppose the lion is really approaching the woman as she sleeps, or is the lion part of the woman's dream? Explain.

Do you think a scene like this could take place in real life? Why or why not?

At-Home Activity: Fantastic Places

The painter, Henri Rousseau, never actually traveled to deserts or jungles or faraway places. Instead, he pictured distant lands while painting in his art studio in Paris, France, or walking through the city's gardens and zoo. He invented these dreamlike scenes of animals and people living in perfect harmony from his imagination.

Did you ever travel to places in your dreams that you've never been to in real life? Close your eyes and travel to an imaginary land where people and animals act in ways that would be impossible in real life. Maybe this is a place where pigs talk like people or horses fly. Invent your own fantasy story about animals and people, and draw your idea.

Henri Rousseau. *The Sleeping Gypsy*. 1887. Oil on canvas, 51″ x 6′7″ (129.5 x 200.7 cm). Gift of Mrs. Simon Guggenheim

The Sleeping Gypsy HENRI ROUSSEAU

At-Home Activity:
Animal Memories

The artist, Marc Chagall, grew up in a small Russian village where people and animals lived close together. Goats, cows, and chickens roamed through backyards and along the unpaved streets. People called the animals by name and depended on them for food, work, and sometimes for friendship. They also believed animals had souls just like humans. When Chagall painted this picture, he was remembering his childhood village. As you can see, he also used his imagination to create a world where people and animals seem to connect with each other in a magical space.

Do you live with any animals? How do you communicate or talk to each other? What kinds of activities do you do together? Draw a picture of special memories that you and the animals in your life share. If you don't have a pet, draw an animal you would like to have.

Look at the entire painting and some of the details, then make up a story about what's happening.

What do you make of the man with the green face? What do you think he is doing?

What can you tell about the animal with the huge head? What do you suppose this animal is thinking?

How do you think the man and the animal feel about each other? What makes you say that?

Find a woman who is upside-down. What do you think she is doing? What other unusual things are happening in this picture?

Imagine being in this picture. What would that be like?

Where do you think this scene is taking place? Can you tell what season or time of day it is?

Compare the way this painting looks to the painting you saw by Rousseau. How are they different?

I and the Village

MARC CHAGALL

Marc Chagall. *I and the Village*. 1911. Oil on canvas, 6′3 5/8″ x 59 5/8″ (192.1 x 151.4 cm). Mrs. Simon Guggenheim Fund

Take a close look at this cat. Describe its face. What can you tell about the way the cat feels?

What do you suppose the cat is thinking or dreaming about?

What do you make of the bird? What do you think it is doing in the picture?

What do you think will happen next?

Think of cats you've seen. Does this one look like them or not? Explain.

At-Home Activity:
I Must Be Dreaming!

Have you ever seen a cat with a red heart-shaped nose? Instead of painting things the way they look in the everyday world, the Swiss artist Paul Klee painted what he saw in his imagination and his dreams. In *Cat and Bird*, you can also see what is on the cat's mind.

Did you ever wonder what animals think or dream about? Make a painting or drawing of an animal's dream.

Cat and Bird PAUL KLEE

Paul Klee. *Cat and Bird*. 1928. Oil and ink on gessoed canvas, mounted on wood, 15 x 21″ (38.1 x 53.2 cm). Sidney and Harriet Janis Collection Fund and gift of Suzy Prudden and Joan H. Meijer in memory of F. H. Hirschland

What seems to be happening in this picture?

What animals and creatures can you find in this picture? What are they doing? Where might this be taking place?

Take a close look at the animals. Have you ever seen animals that look like this in real life? Explain.

Find the guitar player. How would you describe this person?

Make up your own title for this painting. Explain your choice.

How is this picture different from the other pictures you've seen so far?

**At-Home Activity:
Create a Creature**

The artist, Joan Miró, grew up in Spain, where he often visited his family's farm. His memories of the farm and the animals that lived there appear in his paintings. Later in his life, he traveled to the Netherlands and then painted scenes of Dutch interiors (or rooms) filled with animals.

As you can see, Miró wasn't interested in painting animals the way they look in real life. Instead, he studied animal forms and changed them into wild and whimsical creatures. Look closely: The animals in his paintings seem to change from one shape to another right before your eyes.

Draw a scene of a room in your home filled with creatures and animals invented from your head. You may want to start by drawing some unusual shapes to get ideas for your creatures.

Dutch Interior, I

JOAN MIRÓ

Joan Miró. *Dutch Interior, I*. 1928. Oil on canvas, 36 ⅛ x 28 ¾" (91.8 x 73 cm). Mrs. Simon Guggenheim Fund

At-Home Activity: Painting Portraits

At Frida Kahlo's home and art studio in Mexico, parakeets, hens, sparrows, deer, a dog, an eagle, and two pet monkeys roamed freely around the garden and even inside the house. In this self-portrait, Kahlo painted herself with her beloved pet monkey Fulang-Chang. Usually we think of monkeys as wild animals, but here the monkey and the woman are close companions. Kahlo holds the monkey like a small child bound to her with a silk ribbon.

Did you ever love an animal as much as a person? How are people like other animals? How are they different? Paint a portrait of yourself with an animal or person you love.

What do you see in this picture? What can you tell about this woman and this monkey?

How do you think the monkey and the woman feel about each other? What makes you say that?

What does her face say about her? What might she be thinking?

What kind of personality do you think the monkey has?

What does the pink ribbon tell you?

Frida Kahlo. *Fulang-Chang and Me*. 1937.
Oil on compostition board, 15 ¾ x 11″ (39.9 x 27.9 cm).
Detail of two-part ensemble assembled after 1939, including painted mirror frame (22 ¼ x 17 ⅜ x 1 ¾″ [56.6 x 44.1 x 4.5 cm]), and accompanying mirror with painted frame (25 ¼ x 19 ⅛ x 1 ¾″ [64.1 x 48.5 x 4.4 cm]).
Mary Sklar Bequest

Fulang-Chang and Me FRIDA KAHLO

Who are these people? What can you tell about them by looking at their clothes? What do you think they are doing?

Who do you think the man holding the reins of the white horse is? What about the man on the ground? Can you tell which man is the hero, Zapata? What makes you say that?

Where do you think this scene is happening? What clues in the picture help you know that?

Describe the horse. Do you think the horse is important in this picture? Why?

At-Home Activity:
Animals from My Country

When the artist, Diego Rivera, was a young child, he lived in the mountains of Mexico. He roamed the forest with his goat, and the animals of the woods became his friends—even the scary ones. The artist once said that he loved animals more than human beings.

Rivera painted this mural to share his country's history. The man holding the horse is Emiliano Zapata, a Mexican hero. Zapata led poor farmers in an uprising against wealthy landowners. By having control of the horse, he shows strength and power. Rivera admired Zapata's courage and considered him a great leader.

What animals are important in your country's history? Which animals, if any, are symbols for your country? Draw a picture that tells a story about animals and the place where you live.

Agrarian Leader Zapata

DIEGO RIVERA

Diego Rivera. *Agrarian Leader Zapata*. 1931. Fresco, 7′9 ¾″ x 6′2″ (238.1 x 188 cm). Abby Aldrich Rockefeller Fund

At-Home Activity:
If I Were an Animal

One day, the artist, Alberto Giacometti, was walking down a rainy street in Paris with his head down, feeling unhappy. He remembered a sad looking dog he had once seen on the street. He felt like a sad dog just then, too. When he returned to his art studio, he quickly sculpted a dog out of plaster. The plaster dog stayed in his studio for eight years before he cast it in bronze.

If you were to draw yourself as an animal, what animal would you choose? What kind of personality would it have? Would it be cuddly or cold, frightened or fierce, shy or outgoing, kind or mean? Make a drawing or sculpture of an animal that is like you.

Describe this dog. How do you suppose this dog feels? What makes you say that?

What can we tell by looking at the dog's body and the way it is posed?

If you saw a dog like this on the street, what would you think about it?

In what ways does the dog seem to be exaggerated or distorted?

The artist once said that this sculpture was like a portrait of himself. What do you suppose he is telling us about himself?

How is *Dog* different from the other artworks you have seen today?

Dog ALBERTO GIACOMETTI

Alberto Giacometti. *Dog*. 1951. Bronze (cast 1957), 18 x 39 x 6 ⅛" (45.7 x 99 x 15.5 cm), including base. A. Conger Goodyear Fund

How would you describe the goat's body and head? What about its belly?

What kind of personality do you think this goat has? What makes you say that?

The artist built the goat out of materials he found, and then cast the sculpture in bronze. Try to identify any objects that were used to create the goat's form. Can you find a part of the goat that was cast from two jugs?

Why do you think someone would want to make a bronze statue of a goat?

Compare this goat to Giacometti's *Dog*. What, if anything, is the same about the two animals? How are they different?

At-Home Activity: Recycle for Art

The artist, Pablo Picasso, had a lifelong love of animals. At his home in France, monkeys, cats, a dog, and even a pet goat ran free inside the house and outside on the grounds. Picasso constructed all sorts of inventive animals and creatures from things he found in his everyday environment. On your next trip to the Museum, look for other animal sculptures by Picasso. You might find a bull made from scraps of wood and a baboon whose head is cast from a toy car!

With an adult, collect throwaway materials such as cardboard rolls and boxes, egg cartons, plastic bottles and other odds and ends from around your home. Work together to construct an animal out of the materials. Use masking tape to assemble the objects. Then carefully wrap the entire form with papier-mâché or plaster of paris. When it's dry, you can paint it.

Pablo Picasso. *She-Goat*. 1950. Bronze (cast 1952), after an assemblage of palm leaf, ceramic flowerpots, wicker basket metal elements and plaster, 46 3/8 x 56 3/8 x 28 1/8" (117.7 x 143.1 x 71.4 cm), including base. Mrs. Simon Guggenheim Fund

She-Goat PABLO PICASSO

At home, create your own Art Safari by following some of the suggested activities. You can draw your ideas on the pages at the end of this book. Remember: There are as many possibilities for art as ideas in your head. Every artist has his or her own way of making things, and as you can see from looking at paintings and sculptures in the Museum, a work of art doesn't have to look "real" to be good. Be inventive, try new ways of seeing things, and don't be afraid to make mistakes. Your own art is whatever you decide to make it. Anything you imagine or feel or think about can be part of your art.